Publishing Your Research in Scholarly Journals.

A street fighter's guide

Richard Croucher

February, 2015

PREFACE

I would like to thank a number of my colleagues at Middlesex University Business School London who kindly took the time and trouble to read and comment on earlier versions of the manuscript. They are: Professor Paul Gooderham, Professor Anne-Wil Harzing, Dr Lilian Miles, Dr Daniel Ozarow. I also thank Mark Houssart for his invaluable help as academic editor in preparing the final manuscript. The usual caveats apply.

I should be grateful for any feedback readers might wish to give.

CONTENTS

3. ALTERNATIVE OUTLETS

   -Working papers

   -Books (texts; monographs; edited books and chapters; theses)

   -Practitioner/popular publications

4. FLY SOLO OR COLLABORATE?

5. DEVELOPING YOURSELF AS A JOURNAL-ORIENTED PUBLISHER

6. TYPES OF SCHOLARLY JOURNAL ARTICLE; ADVANTAGES AND HAZARDS

   -Review articles

   -Theoretical articles

   -Method articles

-Testing or extending theory against empirical evidence articles

-Empirical articles

-Policy articles

-Discussion and debate articles

-Research notes

7. ARTICLE CONCEPTION AND POSITIONING

8. DRAFTING THE ARTICLE: THE PROCESS

9. SIGNIFIERS OF A STRONG ARTICLE

10. SIGNIFIERS OF A WEAK ARTICLE

11. SUBMITTING THE ARTICLE

12. RECEIVING AND RESPONDING TO JOURNAL FEEDBACK

-Introduction

-Rejection

-Revise and re-submit

13. PUBLICISING YOUR ARTICLE

14. REFERENCES

Introduction

The purpose of this short book is to help all those who are interested in publishing their research in scholarly journals or who are already doing that and wish to improve their performance. It draws on my personal experience over many years as an editor of scholarly journals, a member of the *British Journal of Management*'s editorial board and the author of over seventy articles in American and European journals. More particularly I have ten years' experience as Director of Research in a large British business school and therefore read and comment on colleagues' articles on a regular basis. I have published work in business and management, law, education, history and sociology.

The book will be especially useful to those people who research in social science, business and management, law, education or history. Although researchers who work in other areas should also benefit from it, you should be aware that I have no experience of publishing in the fields of literature, natural science or mathematics.

My aim is to provide a systematic and practical combination of advice and tips in a grounded way based on my experience and taking a pragmatic rather than a purist approach: hence 'a street fighter's guide'. The results are likely to be relevant to researchers of all levels of experience. The book is therefore designed to help all academics including those with experience of the processes and ideas introduced here. However, it is obvious that those with less experience stand to gain more from reading it. One sub-group of the wider population who might find it especially useful is those people who are making the transition from having earned their doctorate to being practising academic researchers, or are practitioners who would like to publish their work in some form including in practitioner publications (I use the term 'early career academics' here). Many people in this sub-group make the assumption that having a doctorate is the end of the academic road when in reality it simply marks the end of apprenticeship and hopefully the beginning of a long period of professional practice. Doctoral theses are judged as student work. Journal publication on the other hand is judged by harsher standards because it involves peer review (which might better be called 'competitor review') by other academics passing judgement under conditions of anonymity. They will decide, together with journal editors, whether you have anything serious to contribute and whether it is something that other academics would like to read. That is quite a different standard. Where top rated journals are concerned, it will be a demanding one and everyone needs help in meeting it.

Accumulating experience in this area is normally a slow process as few people submit more than two articles a year to scholarly journals. Since it will probably take between one and two years for those articles to appear in print, acquiring direct experience across a range of journals and types of article will necessarily be slow. In the meantime, people will be exposed to the reported experiences of their immediate colleagues but these may well be filtered and not give a rounded picture, making them positively unhelpful to some researchers. I well remember, from my time as an undergraduate, students who claimed to do very little work who also had top marks; it was considered the height of coolness. Other processes are at work with colleagues' feedback. Universities contain many wonderfully collaborative people genuinely interested in helping their colleagues' careers. They also include other types of people.

Everything in this book is simply one individual's advice and reflects my personal experience and subjective judgements; I hope that others provide their own perspectives to provide a fuller set of written views in an area dominated by sometimes confusing and contradictory verbal folklore and half-baked stories. It is based on experience accumulated as an author, editor, reviewer and adviser of colleagues over twenty years. In the past ten years I have read and commented on an average of at least one paper per week from colleagues. All of my advice is debatable and many have decided to contest it. There have been many occasions when junior colleagues have told me that my advice is wrong or misleading and they intend going their own way. I do note though that none of them have ever come back to tell me triumphantly that they their work has been published in the top-rated journals they were targeting. There is no one right way to become a successful publishing academic but starting out with specific starting points in mind may help you. What is offered here is largely heuristics or rules of thumb to help you make your own judgements.

Certain personal qualities are required to publish in top scholarly journals on a consistent basis year in, year out. Some people imagine that all that is needed is to be a member of a particular academic network, to use certain tricks or to do everything described in this book, but that is incorrect. The precondition is the capacity to practice your discipline(s) and/or fields of study, including the ability to structure and construct arguments to a high standard in the English language. After this scholarly precondition has been met, the first requirement is consistent hard work. My emotions when I am writing an article often swing between high levels of enthusiasm and optimism and the reverse, sometimes linked to many other contextual things in my life. I have learned that this is normal at least for me and that the key thing is just to keep on working whichever mood I am in. The second quality that is needed, in the immortal words of quite an eminent professor of my acquaintance, is 'a hide like a f...... rhinoceros'. That will help a lot in dealing with the disappointments, frustrations and put-downs you will certainly receive.

You will also need to have good time management and discipline as part of a sharp focus on research and writing.

Many academics at the beginning of their careers have to be preoccupied with their teaching, which (along with administrative work) makes immediate and often unpredictable demands when new courses have to be mastered and delivered. As a result, it is all too easy for new academics to let their research and writing slide. It may be postponed to some indeterminate point in the future which in some cases never arrives. Writing articles does require a certain momentum: if in the initial ground-breaking stage an article is not worked on most days of the week then when I start again, I constantly have to waste time picking up almost from the very beginning again. Working like this is occasionally inevitable but little progress is made. Part of the trick here is to be able to use ten minutes, not just ten hours. Ten minutes can be used to check a reference or refine a sentence. It is normally possible to snatch short periods like that most days. It maintains momentum and means that your sub-conscious is working much of the time.

Overall, I argue here that it is precisely because writing for scholarly publication is largely and essentially an individual process, success is likely to come from recognising and leveraging its social aspects. My suggestions are not limited to the social dimensions, but they are fundamental to success. I stress the importance of learning from your peers, networking in scholarly environments, participating in and managing collaborations, publicising and diffusing your work effectively and so on. Social reciprocity and the idea of a collective enterprise rather than an individualistic outlook based on an instrumental view of other academics is central to my outlook.

The book does not attempt to do certain things. It is not a research methods primer, of which there is a large number in the different fields encompassed by this work and especially in social science and the fields of study based on it. My assumption is that the research has essentially been done and the data are collected. It is evident that you will need to have identified an area with a research gap, to have used sound methods and have work with the potential for making a serious contribution. Bluntly put, nothing can be achieved without first doing good research. The processes, approaches and tips outlined here cannot compensate for doing poor research. Research can sometimes go off the rails and I recommend consulting Streiner and Sidani (2010) if that happens.

What follows is organised in sections that, although they are based on the sequence in many article-writing processes, are also necessarily artificial as many sections overlap and in some cases occur in the wrong order if you are writing a certain type of article.

Why publish in scholarly journals?

It is very important for you to establish in your own mind exactly why you are embarking on publishing in scholarly journals, or indeed publishing at all. Doing so is central to ensuring that when you wake up at night (or cannot sleep in the first place) because of the problems you are wrestling with, that you have a good answer—i.e. one that convinces you rather than someone else—to the question of why you are doing it.

There are clear external, career reasons for most academics to be interested in publishing their work. In North American, British and to an increasing extent in Continental European and Asian universities it has become near-essential to obtaining a first academic position and also to progressing within the academic profession. There are some institutions in which this has not taken a firm hold, but even in them, the wind of change is blowing hard because the institution's reputation (and ability attract students in a competitive world) depends on staff prowess as shown by peer-reviewed research outputs. If those with shiny doctorates do obtain positions without having proven their capacity to publish, they will always in a sense be 'on probation' in the eyes of their peers and certainly of their managers, however good they are at the essential and honourable task of teaching. Once a position has been obtained, progress up the academic ranks via internal or external promotion is unlikely without publication in the better journals unless you specialise in very specific managerial or leadership roles and demonstrate outstanding capacity in them. Even in that case, most universities will not award professorial titles to those who have not published seriously in places that convince the university's professoriate. This is simply because they have no professional credibility in an academic institution.

In many universities, peer expectations are at least as important as managerial pressure to inducing academics to show what they can do in the research and publication area. One important reason for many people publishing their research is so that they can hold their heads up high among their peers. A reason for carrying on through all of the difficulties is often that their collaborators need them to do their work and many academics feel that peer pressure keenly.

However, all of these reasons are external to the individual and unlikely to be enough on their own to motivate them sufficiently to undertake these demanding activities. 'Because other people want it' is rarely as powerful a motivator as 'because I want it'. It is noticeable that some academics still seem to imagine that they need only operate within the framework of a standard working week to publish their work, but this is unlikely to succeed. Research and writing are very labour-intensive operations that mean that people have to work all hours to carry them out in any volume and with any degree of success. This in turn means that the motivation to do them almost certainly needs to be strong and intrinsic: you do it because you want to and because you appreciate the intrinsic rewards of finding things out and sharing the results with others. Without that sort of motivation, given the difficulties, it is unlikely to work across a long period.

This still leaves the question of why you want to publish your work in scholarly journals rather than submerge yourself in research and writing processes and seek publication by less demanding routes. It may be simply because you feel you have something that you want to say. One journal editor who had helped me to publish quite an obscure article in an equally obscure and not very well-rated journal once articulated this very accurately in my case: 'You needed to get that off your chest, didn't you?' was his very accurate comment. Another reason that many put forward is 'because I want to make a difference'. In the case of policy research this may be possible to achieve; it is not unheard of for senior public servants to be quite well-informed about academic literature and what you write may impact their thinking. Moreover, partly thanks to electronic methods of distribution and dissemination, academic articles are sometimes quite widely read. Their audiences are not always as small as some people argue or imagine as it is not uncommon for some academic articles to have paid downloads exceeding the sales of the average academic book. On the other hand, even if an idea has a lot of resonance with certain audiences, it will probably need to be disseminated beyond the pages of scholarly journals (for example through practitioner publications and/ or books, radio, television and on-line media) if it is to make much difference. At the end of this book, I discuss methods of disseminating your work in much more detail.

Dissemination of research results and ideas is a worthwhile activity in a general, social sense and there are outstanding cases where academics have changed the terms of public discussion internationally. An outstanding example is that of Thomas Piketty whose now very well-known work *Capital in the Twenty First Century* was preceded and heralded by a series of articles in scholarly journals. When his major book was launched, many scholars were already aware of his arguments concerning long-term trends in wealth, inequality and taxation. The publication of his book brought debate in many serious newspapers such as the *Financial Times* (including a failed attempt to undermine his findings) and changed the way that many thought about these subjects.

Alternative outlets

I now consider the alternatives or, better put, complements to publishing in scholarly journals. They have their respective merits and all deserve a place in a personal publication strategy. I think of these as: conference papers, working papers, books of different types and practitioner publication. Practitioner publication should not be ignored or dismissed. It may be very effective at advancing certain types of academic career that have a significant practice element, and this type of publication may well draw on experience, and/or on a vocational doctorate.

Once you know why you are publishing a particular work, you are in a better position to decide on how you want to publish it because the means should suit the ends. The typical way for academics is to begin by writing a conference paper, in the hope that s/he will be able to present it and to receive feedback from others while they are networking among significant figures in their fields, journal editors and peers. If this is to be very effective, then the first requirement is that the conference itself be a reasonably good one. The academic world has been flooded by conferences, many of which are simply or at least little more than money-making operations whereby universities pay for academics to visit pleasant destinations and exchange papers. The reviewing processes in these cases are often laughable; they may allow individuals to say on their publications lists that they are 'refereed' but the processes involved are not rigorous. The same is likely to apply to the conference itself, where discussion may not be quite what you had hoped for. When we consider the opportunity cost to the academic, who in some cases might have been able to draft a paper in the time taken to fly across the world, attend a lengthy conference, fly back again and recover, the activity is of very questionable value. Certain conferences on the other hand are a very different proposition and promise to be valuable experiences. The views and experiences of experts in each specific field should be sought to decide which type of conference is in question.

Working papers may be an alternative to conference papers and many universities have useful working paper series. These are typically papers which present the first stages of an analysis or argument, which are put in the public domain to present these early findings prior to a more developed publication at a later stage. In some subjects such as economics, working papers have a particularly strong tradition and are often widely cited. The clear advantage of this interim type of publication is that it gets findings out quickly. Working papers are normally also internally refereed, providing the author with friendly reviews. They are typically then posted on the web and in some cases printed in a simple form. They may also be edited by an editor internal to the institution. You need to be extremely careful with this form of publication for more than one reason. The first is that ideas might be taken and worked up by some unscrupulous people. Second and more importantly, many scholarly journals and especially well-rated North American outlets run submitted articles through sophisticated software. This software will likely pick up at least parts of your web-published working paper. Your submitted article will then be returned to you with a sharp rejection note from the editor. You will have been accused of 'self-plagiarism', an accusation that is likely to herald the end of the article's future. 'Self-plagiarism' is not something anyone wants to acquire a reputation for, and of course is also something to look out for more widely than with working papers.

Books are another clear alternative to journal publication. Monographs and indeed books in general can also allow different audiences to be reached than journal articles although this is not always the case at least in terms of simple numbers as many academic books sell between 400 and 1000 copies and more than a few articles achieve at least this level of paid downloads. They are especially common at the beginning and end of individuals' careers in the first case for publicity and in the second for valedictory purposes. There are different types of book to be considered: text books, monographs, edited books and minimally-edited theses. I now deal with these four varieties in turn.

The first is text books. The advantages of writing text books are probably mainly that they link to people's teaching and that they may be heavily used and bought in large numbers. In these ways, the authors can diffuse their ideas to students and raise their profile in a lot of institutions. The disadvantage is that there will be many requirements from publishers about format and establishing a case for a new text book in what may be a crowded market. Very often, publishers require accompanying exercises and so on to be prepared for the web and linked in to the publication. These often take up a lot of time and energy. More important for our purposes, even when they have some basis in the author's research, they are simply not rated in universities as research outputs. There is therefore also a very real opportunity cost to this kind of activity.

A second type of book, the monograph, allows authors to present extended treatments of subjects in ways that journal articles do not and is much more likely than text books to be taken seriously as a research output. It is in this area that the differences between disciplines become most apparent. In some areas, such as law, history and education, they may (depending, of course, on the book itself) be very well regarded. In law, history and education, books are seen as the main way of establishing individuals' reputations. In these subjects, it is rare to appoint a senior member of staff without a book to their name. Consequently, in these disciplines, the choice of publisher is a real issue: who published it? The famous university presses, although they sometimes publish books of dubious merit and not always in good order, remain the benchmark here. Books published by these companies usually have to go through an initial reviewing process not dissimilar to that which journal articles go through. It is important to ensure that the publisher has established criteria: they are therefore primarily commercial rather than academic (will it sell in the USA?). Publishing is a business. The publisher is first and foremost concerned with the book project's commercial viability and particularly the size of the world-wide audience. Therefore, book proposals consisting of a proposal, an outline of how the contents will be structured and a sample chapter are reviewed (often very well) from this viewpoint. Also, from an academic perspective, texts even from some of the large and famous university presses too often appear without having been properly edited or proof-read and their formatting, production and printing can also sometimes leave something to be desired. My advice to all authors is to treat the services offered by all publishers as supplements to their own efforts rather than as substitutes for them. Do not rely on the publisher, however reputable.

Rather than write a research monograph, it may be that a third possibility, editing a collection of chapters written by others around a theme, is attractive to yourself and to a publisher. It allows you to network very constructively on the basis of mutual utility to yourself and to those you are working with, because you are likely to ask people already accomplished in a particular field to contribute. Whether they accept or deliver even approximately to deadline is another matter of course. Generally speaking, you will need as a book (or journal) editor to build in a margin for non-delivery to the required standard. It is important though to realise from the outset that although good relations with authors may be built, alternatively they may suffer if they agree and then let you down. Sometimes, contributors expect editors to make sure their texts are brought up to the required standard if they are criticised by others. Deadlines, as I indicated above, are also often an issue. When I recently contributed a chapter to an edited book of some twenty chapters just before the deadline, one of the editors told me that I was the first to do so. What is more, some authors are reluctant to accept critical comment or to have their drafts edited at all. The editors—like all editors--are engaged in trying to improve the author's work and with it their reputation, but some authors are too self-important to accept that and simply reject suggestions. In these cases, the positive networking effects may be reduced or even removed. This type of friction can mean that the effort and cost of co-ordinating others makes you wish you had written the book yourself. You might consider responding positively to an invitation from a colleague to contribute a chapter to an edited book, something that has similar advantages to writing other non-refereed publications in that you can 'let your hair down' a bit more and achieve publication at the same time. You should be aware though, that since chapters are not peer-reviewed, they do not carry a lot of prestige even when you find you are in good company with the book editors and contributors.

A fourth type of book publication is also an option. Some specialist publishers have started to publish doctoral and master's dissertations with minimal editing on the web. As this often involves the author in very little work, it has the real advantage that your results are put in the public domain relatively quickly and painlessly. The old practice, common in continental Europe, of recent doctoral theses simply being sent to publishers and hoping that they will be considered for publication has almost completely died out. Even the more academic publishers require authors to make many fundamental changes to a thesis before they will consider it as a potential book. The thesis is a very different form from the book, with very different requirements. Despite the normal stipulation that PhDs should be in principle publishable, some doctoral theses in reality may not be suitable for publication: expert advice should be taken. Moreover, there may well be issues with 'self-plagiarism' from the thesis when you come to submit work from it to a journal, of which more below.

Practitioner or popular publications are other useful outlets you should consider. There is a wide range of types of publication in this area. Many present a mix of news, ideas, magazine items and the results of research in a more journalistic way to a wide but specific audience. Examples from business and management include magazines such as *People Management* and newspapers such as the *Financial Times*; in history, *History Today* is an equivalent; in education, the *Times Educational Supplement* or specialist subject associations have a similar function. This sort of publication has a number of advantages for us as researchers. First, in common with book chapters, it may be a useful preparatory exercise for the initial marshalling of material and ordering of arguments before embarking on an article. Reversing this logic, it might be written after the scholarly article, in which case it will need to be 'de-academicised' before submission. Although there may be something in common, journalism is quite different from academic writing, not simply using different language but following different structural conventions. Second, it is unlikely to take too much time. Third, it allows a non-academic audience to be reached and individuals may well respond, providing the author with potential further data, experiences and arguments. Since all researchers wherever they are have (very properly) to pay attention to reaching wider audiences, this type of publication should almost certainly form part of any well-conceived personal publication strategy. The order in which the different types of publication appear is worth considering; although I have here shown a preference for moving from practitioner to scholarly publication, the reverse order may also be appropriate and even preferable in some circumstances.

Fly solo or collaborate?

Whether to write alone or to work as part of a team is an important decision, especially at the beginning of your research career. The merit of working on your own is obviously that the effort and achievement (if it materialises) is yours and yours alone. It need not mean that you are working *entirely* on your own as others may well be generous enough to comment on your work and even to help in small ways, without requesting co-authorship. A reputation for expertise in a particular field may be built more easily in this way because there is no doubt that you, rather than your co-authors, have done the work. Perhaps the biggest disadvantage is that the author is not receiving so much of the cross-fertilisation of ideas that s/he will receive through collaboration. It is also unlikely that one author, unless they are exceptional, will have all the different capacities required to succeed in getting published in very competitive journals. Almost as important is that if the article is not well-received, there is nobody else to share the pain with, and rejection may lead to a bout of probably exaggerated self-doubt.

Collaboration happens across academe but is practised and seen differently in different disciplines; it is the norm in natural science, social science and business and management but less common in history, law and many other areas; in education, both modes of production are quite usual. Some collaboration is mainly driven by an article's subject matter; international work in any discipline is likely to require it for example. It is normally, and probably should be, especially important at the start of your career, since well-managed collaboration accelerates your development. Collaboration often has huge advantages and the biggest is that you learn from it in all kinds of ways.

How it is initially set up is a serious matter and here I begin by identifying three key issues: the 'offer' of different researchers; authorial group management and finally issues around experience, power and authority. I begin with the 'offer' subject. First of all, one has to establish and build a collaboration and unfortunately some researchers are only dimly aware of how this might be done (one reason for a common reliance on doctoral supervisors). You must have an 'offer' to the other researcher (s) that is attractive to them. Just to be working in the same field does not constitute an offer. The offer may be based on you having good data or access to data, different types of expertise (for an historian, knowledge of a particular individual actor's biography for example; for a business specialist, knowledge of a specific industry), or strong theoretical or writing skills. Of these methods, good quality data is probably the most effective. Data itself can be circulated to groups of researchers you trust or even published as part of a search for collaborators; ethics dictate that since this is your data you must be named as co-author. Whatever the basis, it needs to be clearly visible to the others involved.

Second, it involves those most difficult of skills and qualities, dealing with people in general and managing the dynamics in small groups in particular. Some small groups work and some simply do not. Friendships may suffer through collaboration. Academics may have the required scientific skills but they can also lack the interpersonal skills needed to manage collaborations. Some are properly called toxic individuals. It is possible, but more difficult, to collaborate with people who you do not like. There are a lot of interactions bringing people into close (and often critical) contact. Someone in the authorial group needs the skills required to ensure the group's effective operation, smooth over any inter-personal difficulties, take the sting out of disagreements, show emotional intelligence and so on. These qualities can be very valuable, but it is hard to claim them as part of your 'offer' to other researchers until you have shown them in practice. Nonetheless, they can potentially make an authorial group into a genuine team which can achieve more than the sum of its parts. This is a difficult thing to achieve and takes a lot of time, but it is an excellent goal for any authorial group.

Bigger groups (possibly coming from funded projects) may need more management. In the humanities, two authors is common. In social science, business and management, larger teams more so. In my experience, groups of four or five are ideal when difficult target journals are concerned, as they can contain sufficient expertise and cohesion is not too difficult to achieve. When authorial groups become too large, typically beyond six, it is likely that some 'free-riding' is going on, sometimes bringing internal tensions. The language of 'inclusion' and 'inclusive approaches' may sometimes be used to justify large authorial groups. Individuals may need reminding that inclusion carries responsibilities.

Third, there are always questions about the experience and capacities available in the authorial group and the power and authority relations involved. For early-career researchers, their supervisors are often the obvious collaborators (see my comments on this elsewhere). There can be drawbacks to collaborating with them. Where supervisors are co-authors and especially if they are very eminent in an area, one has to realise that (whatever the order of authors' names on the publication) many will see the work as theirs rather than yours. Unfair as it may be, this is the reality. Another, more unusual, difficulty that can arise is where a supervisor takes rather an unusual view (for example of appropriate methods) and propagates that among his doctoral students, who later find that journals do not accept that idiosyncratic approach. Supervisors can play an inordinately large role in a doctoral student's life, but the supervisor may well not reflect the subject's mainstream or even subscribe to generally-accepted approaches. Journals may be seen in some senses as enforcers of conformity. Therefore, at some point, you will need to break out on your own or work with other collaborators. In any case, at a certain point one needs to leave home and not simply be seen as someone else's disciple however wonderful they may be. Some supervisors are very well-connected and may be able to help you to network effectively, so disciple-ship may have some advantages, but it is also a state that is probably best transcended at some point as you will want to establish your own individual scholarly identity.

Sometimes, there is a feeling among early career researchers that they need to establish themselves with an absolute minimum of involvement from more senior colleagues. They may therefore work together without any senior researcher participation. This has all the (very real) advantages of egalitarianism including a lack of formal hierarchy, but it also clearly means that the team lacks significant experience and generally suffers as a result. It is likely to take longer for the group to accumulate the experience they need to operate effectively.

If we assume that all of these matters have been settled, how to take the collaboration further and manage it through to a successful conclusion? Managing collaborators and collaborations is as complicated as managing people, and it is difficult to do more than to suggest some principles; I now suggest four. The first is that the most successful collaborations in terms of the quality of the articles they produce are almost certainly those which involve a lot of face-to-face interactions. While it is clearly possible to work together by e-mail, video conferences and so on this does not allow for the type of interaction where one talks casually and freely. In my experience, these interactions often lead to the best ideas. Face-to-face interactions allow for a lot more of the 'talk-write-talk-write' approach (meaning a constant interaction between the verbal and written forms of expression, I give more details below) that we advocate in this book. A second principle is to try to create collaborations where the individuals' skills are complementary rather than similar. This way, a more rounded result is likely. A third principle, where senior-junior collaboration is involved, is for both parties (but probably in reality the senior one in particular) to make explicit the key learning points as the work proceeds. In other words, to say things like 'we need to ensure that all tables are properly labelled in all of our work' as required. This will speed up the learning process and if it is initially agreed and accepted between the parties it can work well. A few minutes should probably be taken at the beginning of the collaboration to make the purpose of this practice clear. All concerned benefit from this type of approach provided it is not delivered or received in a bad-tempered way. Very often, it is less a matter of learning something entirely new (and therefore my example might appear too banal and obvious). It is more a matter of reminding ourselves of old or well-known lessons that we have not fully embedded in our everyday practice because of the wide range of tasks we have to perform when writing an article.

A fourth principle is that authorship should be dealt with in an equitable and collegial way; I will now spend some time discussing this important element. Authorship is a subject that looms large in collaboration. It has long struck me that although universities have numerous ethics committees, very little of their time appears to be taken up with the ethics of authorship, though there are often a lot of colleagues complaining in private about them. Of course, there is the underlying issue of what constitutes authorship. At what point does commenting on and/or editing an article cross the line into an entitlement to be named as a co-author? Many have discussed this issue in more erudite ways than myself, but my basic criterion is that the following jobs merit more than an acknowledgement: (a) Contributing data (b) Contributing more than one significant argument or interpretation (c) Contributing more than a few references (d)Contributing a significant re-framing of an article or a section of the article. What does not constitute co-authorship and is in my view potentially unethical is when someone claims co-authorship or allows him or herself to be named as co-author simply because the individual is a young academic's supervisor or ex-supervisor.

In collaborative work, the order of authors' names can become an issue or, even worse, can simply be assumed. On several occasions, I have been surprised that some academics have made a huge issue of being the first-named author and even pushed the matter quite hard, sometimes for immediate career reasons but always to the detriment of team relationships. The conventional way of listing authors is in strict alphabetical order of family names, unless one author has made an inordinate contribution. In the disciplines and fields of study dealt with in this book, it is normal for the first-named author to be considered the prime mover and the person who can claim the most credit for a work. However, in the era of cross-disciplinary work, it is worth being aware that in some disciplines, such as natural science, the reverse is true. After the first author, the order of names is often not thought to be important until one comes to the last author, normally seen as the least significant (except in the natural sciences).

Sometimes, teams of authors try to avoid any problems arising later on by determining the order of authors' names at the outset. In some cases this may be possible and in those cases it will at least minimise the chances of rancorous disputes breaking out at the end of the process. To remove all doubt, some authorial teams state their policy in a footnote at the beginning of their articles. The issue, however, is that the extent to which individuals have contributed cannot be determined before the end of the process-the end of the process being not the point of initial submission, but the point at which the article is finally accepted, which may be several revisions down the line. At this point, it may feel too late to change the order agreed at the point of initial submission.

All of these issues are tricky and are probably most easily dealt with where the authorial group has a good stream of work and can operate a system of allowing for different people's contributions (and needs) to be recognised in ways that reflect an entire stream of work rather than an individual publication.

Developing yourself as a journal-oriented publisher

Becoming an independent journal-oriented academic, publishing regularly in good quality journals, is a process that takes most individuals a few years after completing their doctorate. They may, as many supervisors encourage students to do, have published an article or two (possibly in one of the lightly-reviewed university-based journals) while writing their thesis but will still need more time to develop. After such a period, you should be a full practitioner rather than an apprentice. This period can be shortened but in the great majority of cases not beyond a certain point. The skills have to be learned across substantial periods of time and it is difficult to shorten the process. Indeed, part of the pleasure in being an academic is that one is always learning. In this section, some suggestions are made about how best to manage this continuing developmental process.

The first and perhaps most obvious way of furthering your development as a researcher is likely to be some sort of mentoring in which you are helped by a more experienced colleague to maximise the benefits of your experience. It will be important here to clarify the formal arrangements—if any—of the institution you work in. The degree of formality varies considerably between universities. Some have a requirement that all staff have mentors; others are much looser in their approach. In reality, there is a continuum of arrangements in most institutions from a very intense relationship which exceeds the level of contact normal in collaboration through to a very weak and probably occasional one where little happens. The question is therefore what it consists of and how it works. Whatever the degree of formalisation, it is likely to work best if at the outset there is discussion between those concerned as to what the content, level and boundaries of the mentoring relationship are to be. On occasions, when mentoring others, I have been surprised by the level of demands made by colleagues, sometimes without any apparent concern for my own schedule or activities. This potentially threatens the relationship. It is a matter of feeling your way here, but an initial discussion about what both parties feel is appropriate in the circumstances is likely to help. In my view, it is important to remember that the long or medium-term aim is learning rather than any specific output. It is also about helping you rather than substituting for your own effort. But this is one subjective view and it may not be shared by the other party, who may come from a culture in which such relationships carry very different meanings.

Mentoring is normally an individual relationship, but wider networks are clearly vital in advancing both academic careers in general and publication in particular. What is needed are high-trust relationships are needed, in which you do what you say, reciprocate favours and show a commitment to 'going the extra mile' for others. Networking in one sense begins at home. Good, open and honest relationships with the scholars around us are a solid basis for building on; invaluable information is available through our colleagues. Unfortunately, these relationships can often be based as much on rivalry as on developing a sense of collective enterprise, but you can try to overcome this and hopefully your colleagues will respond positively. More widely, academics need to be part of at least one wider scholarly community with whom they share some definable research interests and concerns, what some people call a 'tribe'. Members of the tribe are likely to attend the same conferences, publish in the same journals and address broadly similar questions in their work. It may be difficult to establish useful communications with the whole of the tribe, but building good relations with sub-groups within it is likely to be easier and fruitful. For example, one can send individuals positive feedback on their published work and, conversely, send them your own work with a request for feedback. In some cases, there will be no response, but in others there may be some reply that can lead to fruitful exchanges and even collaborations.

Some of these subject-oriented networks are institutionalised in the form of well-established scholarly societies with excellent reputations and close links to well-regarded journals (the Economic History Society with its prestigious journal *Economic History Review* is an example) and their own book series (the Society for the Study of Labour History's *Studies in Labour History* is a case in point). The societies may provide a route on to the editorial board of their journals. These societies run conferences on their own and in collaboration with other organisations, and may have a branch or regional structure running a seminar series (such as the British Universities' Industrial Relations Association's branch series). It may be worth looking for the relevant societies in your field. These scholarly societies can provide invaluable networking opportunities for academics. They can also enable them to make themselves useful and even indispensable to members of their 'tribe' outside of their institution. Many essential jobs and roles within them are not much sought after and everyone is grateful to anyone who will do them: in the days when people used overhead projectors anyone who would carry them around a conference was invaluable. Rather more onerous jobs like Treasurer also attract gratitude and might not be too much work. The danger with certain scholarly societies is that they are sometimes made up of 'in' and 'out' groups and even factions based on different research paradigms ('he's one of those number-crunchers') or politics. Being pushed into one camp or another in these situations can make the society as a whole rather dysfunctional and membership of a faction may actually cause you and your work to be regarded sceptically by members of other factions.

The principle of trying to make yourself useful to your colleagues is also applicable to involvement in scholarly journals. One of the problems (it is in some cases *the* problem) faced by journal editors is finding enough reviewers to provide good quality reviews while meeting deadlines. That is one reason why relatively inexperienced academics and even doctoral students are sometimes asked to review articles, an offer that should be accepted. If that does not just happen, it should be possible to make it happen. Anyone letter to the editor offering to review articles in that way, specifying the individual's area of expertise together with some illustration of how that has been demonstrated is unlikely to find its way into the editor's recycle bin unless the mail is poorly constructed and full of spelling mistakes. In due course, when the reviewer is better-established with the editor, that individual can make themselves invaluable by offering to write good reviews quickly when the editor is in a fix. This happens when editors are let down badly by reviewers and are being pressurised for a quick response (usually after long delays) by prestigious article authors.

There are other roles that journals find difficult to fill. One is book reviews editor, simply because journals find it difficult to find anyone willing to provide book reviews. Yet the book reviews editor has an 'offer' that can be attractive to some other academics, being able to provide a pristine copy of a hot from the press book (academic books can of course be very expensive) in return for a review written to a template. A good book reviews section can greatly enhance a journal's usefulness to academics especially in those disciplines in which books are important ways of disseminating new knowledge. In these ways, researchers can earn an editor's gratitude, something likely to be useful to them in the long term.   Later on in your career you can try more ambitious initiatives. Applying to edit a special edition of a journal in your field is the most important. Being a journal editor is a relentless task, even for journals that publish only a small number of editions annually; to be able to simply allocate a whole edition to guest editors is a major relief (although it carries risks, to some extent shared with the guest editors). Therefore, a good application is likely to stand a real chance of acceptance by the general editors.

There are advantages to becoming the editor of a special edition. The first and perhaps the most obvious is that it will enhance your reputation in the field, especially if the special edition is well received by your 'tribe'. The second is that it provides you with valuable editorial experience that in due course may be used to allow you to become a member of an editorial board or an editor. A third reason is that it allows you to strengthen your network and to provide colleagues with a valuable outlet for their work. Fourth, it will give the opportunity to write an editorial introduction, allowing you a significant platform for your ideas although you should be aware that these works are not regarded (sometimes rather unfairly given the work involved and the possibility of critical feedback from the general editors or others) as an article like any other but rather as a 'soft' publication. Nevertheless, there are considerable advantages, although they have to be balanced against the large amount of work involved and of course the risk that some of your peers may find their articles rejected.

How to apply? Some journals specify on their web sites exactly how applications should be made, giving details of what information they require and whom to submit the application to. Many do not, although this does not mean that they will not consider applications. In these cases I recommend the following structure: (1 The title of the special edition with an account of the precise subject area to be covered (this needs to be carefully scoped out and delimited) and specific possible areas for articles (2) A statement about the importance and timeliness of the edition (3) How the special edition fits into recent developments in the journal (4) Relate all of this to any public statements made by the general editorial team about the direction they want to take the journal in (5) How relations with the general editors will be managed (the real question here is how much control you will want to exercise over the edition and how much they will allow you) (6) CVs of the special edition editors, together with statements of their editorial experience (7) A timetable for the production of a complete set of articles in good order and in the journal's required format, and an editorial introduction (with a statement about how this will be reviewed and by whom) and list of contents.

You might consider proposing holding a conference as preparation for a special edition as this has real advantages even if it entails more work. First, it allows for the exchange of ideas and perspectives and induces people to situate themselves in the social context of their area of interest. Second, it helps establish and solidify relationships both between the contributors and between those and the editor(s) which can prevent later difficulties.

You should not underestimate the amount of work it will take to try to obtain good articles, get reviewers, assess their feedback, follow through rounds of revision, write your editorial introduction and finally ensure the special edition is delivered in timely fashion and in the journal's format.

Types of scholarly journal article: advantages and hazards

The choice about what type of article you are going to produce is clearly a fundamental one. There are different types, and your selection should be determined by your article's selling points, your personal strengths and those of the authorial team. It is important to 'play to your strengths', or in other words to lead with what you and others think you are good at. It is also much easier and ultimately more convincing to readers when you write in areas where you either have a strong hinterland of reading and knowledge, or real personal experience. In short, the rule of thumb should be to write about what you know about.

All articles need at least one strong selling point, and preferably more. You need to be strict with yourself in deciding what the selling points of the specific piece of work are. Some of the things people imagine to be 'selling points' are not really 'selling points' at all. You can have different selling points but they MUST be strong and clear to critical readers. The best selling points are probably a genuine theoretical contribution or novel argument, or real topicality. The weakest is 'nobody did this before'. Perhaps nobody did it before because it is of little or no theoretical or wider interest.

I now run through the different types of articles and some of the specific advantages and challenges you are likely to find with each type. Clearly, there are major overlaps between these different 'types' and indeed some articles may contain elements of all of them; it is a question of where the main thrust or selling point of the article lies.

Review articles. Supervisors quite often try to encourage doctoral candidates to attempt these and the next type of article before other types. In the case of review articles this is almost certainly simply because the student usually has a reasonable grasp of the literature (although they often have difficulty in constructing high-quality reviews). There are numerous guides to writing this sort of work (see for example the excellent if rather difficult guide by David Scott, 2012). The general fault with this sort of article is that it amounts to little more than a 'picture gallery' in which various works are described and there is too little attempt to synthesise or to do more than identify a real or supposed 'gap'. Identifying gaps is important but not sufficient. It is also dangerous ('nothing has been written on x.....' someone writes; but if you are wrong, your article is finished as a going concern. Even where your phrasing is careful, you have not done what you should be doing).

Review articles have the considerable advantage of being highly cited by those wanting to point to an overview of a particular area without running through the entire literature in their own article. They require a broad knowledge of the topic area and a strong argument about the strengths and weaknesses of the strand of literature. Increasingly, this type of article is influenced by the 'systematic review' or 'meta-analysis' method imported into the social sciences and business and management from medical science (see the useful article by Tranfield et.al, 2003 outlining the method and its potential in management studies). In the meta-review, a large number of articles are defined in and out of a field and the consensus of opinion across on a key issue is assessed. It is a demanding set of techniques which requires specific training and mastery, but it can also inform reviews that do not use all of its tools.

Theoretical articles. What such an article potentially consists of is not clear to many researchers and some mistakenly see it simply in terms of absence: an article without data. Only a small minority of early career researchers have the capacity to operate at the level of abstraction needed to construct a purely or largely theoretical article.

What is 'theory'? Theory is generalised, abstract propositions about phenomena, their mechanics, causes, consequences and how they inter-relate. Theoretical arguments must be made from valid and reliable existing knowledge and therefore statements must be supported by reference to at least one academically credible source. Arguments may also be made by reference to logic or first principles. Theoretical articles may discuss definitional issues and their consequences for a field, develop a line of argument of fundamental importance, or import a concept from one field and show its relevance and limitations in another. An article may (though it is uncommon to be able to develop this in such a short space) offer a theory explaining a phenomenon at a universal level. More likely, it will at best offer a meso- or micro- level theory. Conceptual clarity and a philosopher-like grasp of argument are at a premium. It is regarded as a high form of the academic's art and is likely to be judged by tough standards. An excellent and quite well-known piece by a previous editor of the *Academy of Management Journal*, David A. Whetten (1989), is still very relevant and offers very good guidance on the theory development process and what he considers a theoretical contribution to be.

Method articles may provide a reflexive account of how you carried out a piece of research. Social scientists have sometimes been accused of being overly preoccupied with research methods (see the article by Jonathan Zeitlin in *Socio-Economic Review*). In the humanities, the reification of method is less common—despite the ravages of post-modernism and the emergence of oral history, historical method remains centred on the principles established by Leopold Ranke in the Nineteenth Century.

An article may raise issues about a particular method in senses that may come close to making it a theoretical article (cite article in *British Educational Research Journal,* around 2006; questioning grounded theory). It might combine methods in a particular way, or propose a new one. These articles can allow you to operate without much data at all, but also require considerable skill, although they are sometimes regarded by some as slightly thin contributions because they are not 'substantive'. They are most common in the social sciences, where there is a strong tradition of this kind of work which you will need to live up to. It is probably not a good idea to write a 'confessional' article (the term is Sara Delamont's) about precisely how and why a research project went wrong at an early point in your career. That may be for later when you have a lot of successful projects to your name.

Testing and/or extending theory against empirical data. This is the most common type of work in social sciences, business and management and is probably what comes immediately to mind for most academics in those fields when the word 'article' is used generically. The idea can be encountered among early career social scientists that using a *specific* method is the key to publication. This is false. Methods should be fit for purpose and the method tail should not wag the investigative dog. The issues with this type of article are often the quality of the theorising, the links between that and the empirics and the conclusions (or, in other words, almost everything). Issues with the quality of the theorising may well be to do with the justification for the hypotheses or propositions for testing. Methods of analysis may of course be problematic, but this is frequently an exaggerated concern in the researcher's mind. A common criticism of this type of article is that the theoretical contribution is absent or too small. Another typical criticism concerns the balance between the theoretical section where hypotheses or propositions are developed for testing and the empirical section. The issue is to show enough theoretical logic to justify or 'motivate' the hypotheses without leaving too little space to present the analysis and draw solid conclusions.

Empirical articles. These are more common in history, education and law than in other areas, as theorising is less highly regarded (and, with due respect to the theorists, arguably less appropriate) in these disciplines than in social science. Nevertheless, it does not mean an article without abstraction. In law, theory is frequently side-lined. By way of illustration, the increasingly beleaguered field of jurisprudence or legal theory (although respected) is now the preserve of a relatively small group of specialists. Articles of this type depend primarily on the depth and detail of the empirics, the quality and originality of the interpretation and of how well they establish the findings' significance. Yet it also requires a good grasp of the relevant literature, a strong argument and interpretive thread running consistently throughout the article, and to establish the importance of the analysis presented.

Policy articles. These examine a particular government or institutional policy and analyse its origins, nature and results with a view to making recommendations to policy makers. They are therefore likely to have an almost in-built strong focus, should not be too difficult to write and can be a good option for ex-practitioners. However, there are also some potential issues. Many articles contain policy recommendations, but these are often divorced from the policy making community's thinking and where this is the case, such recommendations are highly unlikely to be implemented or even taken very seriously. They can also be very time-sensitive as policy may change drastically in a short time. If this type of article is being considered, it will be most effective and almost certainly a better article for close engagement and discussion with the policy community concerned. If you do not have this opportunity it is probably best to make only cautious, tentative and provisional suggestions for policy. If the article is about one country and has no link into policies in other countries then it probably will not appeal to an international journal. It will probably therefore be best to position the article (see below where I discuss positioning in more detail) in a way that makes it relevant beyond one country's borders.

Discussion and debate articles. Some journals have sections where discussion and debate is encouraged through short articles of up to a few thousand words entering into dialogue with other researchers on a specific issue. This is not, as some think, an easy route to publication. The article has to offer a substantial contribution to the debate. It must also be duly respectful of the other discussants. Being a very active protagonist in acerbic debate is unusual for early career researchers for obvious reasons.

Research Notes. These are also short items again of up to a few thousand words, which can take different forms in different disciplines. They frequently make one or two main points. They may present an interesting brief analysis that is related to one theory or, in the case of law, draw attention to a particular case (a 'case note'). In history, it might do the same for a newly-unearthed document or group of documents and their significance. Alternatively, they may in effect be miniature versions of full articles. Editors who feel that a full research article submitted to them is too insubstantial and would be better presented as a research note sometimes invite authors to re-present their work in this form and this is probably the origin of many such pieces. As with contributions to debate items, you should be clear that many do not regard them as full articles and you do need to bear that in mind. Honesty is the best policy in publications lists, and different headings should be used for different article genres.

Article Conception and Positioning

How articles are initially conceived and 'positioned' or located in relation to a subject area or debate is something of great importance and you should take your time in thinking about these matters. All too often, people jump too quickly into writing, before they have thought long and hard about the article's overall conception and positioning. What will be its overall argument, shape and contribution? What will its selling points be to a specialist audience? These questions need to find reasonably clear answers at a very early stage because by asking (and beginning to answer them) at that point, the whole process of writing will become more efficient and take less time than if you only have fuzzy answers. One of the best ways of doing this is to write an initial abstract and I discuss this further below.

The question of positioning is also an important one to answer, preferably at an early stage. 'Positioning' may seem rather an abstract concept, but it refers to which 'conversation' your article is going to contribute to. To give an example from the business and management field, you might have the idea of writing an article about employee behaviour in companies. It is likely that such a piece of work could be positioned in different ways. It might take an organisation studies approach whereby the main questions are about the organisation itself, its routines, rituals and cultures and how these influence employees. It might take an organisational behaviour approach within which the focus is more on broad theories about how people operate in organisations and the consequences of these behaviours for firms of a certain type. Alternatively, it might be participating in a conversation in organisational psychology, using more psychological theories which focus on the employees themselves. It might position itself more in Human Resource Management and discuss how the different types of strategy used to manage labour affect employee behaviour or vice versa. This positioning process needs to take account of where the strengths of the data and the interests of the authorial team lie.

When you are positioning your article, it is a good idea to think about the target journal's audience and, even more importantly, the audience the publishers and editors are currently trying to reach (the journals themselves and colleagues may be able to help you here with information about both). For example, a high proportion of journals have the word 'international' in their title. This may reflect a genuinely international orientation, or alternatively it may reflect a regional (European or North American for example) one. Publishers and editors alike have become far more interested in becoming genuinely international in scope. This has been the case with some journals based in the USA because at one point these were almost exclusively the preserve of US-based authors writing on US-based topics with little awareness of the rest of the world and apparently also very little awareness that researchers ever wrote in languages other than English. Many of these journals are now changing and an increasing number of articles authored by Asian, African and Australian scholars are appearing, on subjects of much broader international interest. This represents an opportunity for some authors. Yet some articles read as though the author (s) have never considered how a reader with only a passing understanding of the situation in a specific country or group of countries might make sense of what they have written. Even if the article is conceived as a policy article (say for example on the effectiveness of a specific national arrangement such as a minimum wage), you should seek to place this in a wider context as many countries have minimum wages and broader policy conclusions may be offered.

You also need to consider how your article will be positioned in relation to your own previous and projected work. It is remarkable how many articles appear to abandon, be in tension with or even contradict arguments put forward by the same author(s) previously. There is obviously no problem with changing perspectives or arguments, but the changes do require some sort of explanation. If difference can be an issue, so too can similarity. You will need to be careful to differentiate one article from another. While a degree of continuity whereby you pick up on previous themes discussed in previous articles may be seen in a positive light, repetition of previous arguments or data with only relatively small nuances of difference is increasingly criticised by reviewers and editors. With the increased pressure on people to publish, authors sometimes try to 'salami slice' their outputs, by bringing out a number of articles with too little difference between them.

Even worse, they may 'self-plagiarise' passages from their own previous works. The latter practice is deeply frowned on by many journal editors, who increasingly use sophisticated software to detect similarities between what is submitted to them and other published work including of course your own. My advice would be even with passages such as method sections that are likely to be identical to those in previous articles, to completely re-word them from previous versions. Similarly with data, some journals object to re-use of the same data; this often seems very unfair since it appears absurd to go to the trouble of collecting certain sorts of large-scale data only to be told that it can only be used once. It is worth taking precautions against this type of accusation by inserting a footnote explaining the different use made of the various variables in a given dataset in the new article. Some journals require this sort of explanation on submission.

Selecting a target journal

In most cases, choosing a target journal early in the process is probably the wisest thing to do so that you know what conversation you are going to contribute to and in a very broad sense how the article will be written. It will also help with questions such as word length and whether footnotes are used rather than Harvard-style references. Changing from one to the other is an arduous task. Choosing a cluster of target journals is an alternative because journals are often grouped around certain themes, and a conversation may have occurred across and beyond the cluster. Sometimes it may not be essential or even advisable to have overly-fixed views about which journal to target until a late stage when the ideas you are discussing in your article take a more definite form; the writing process can sometimes lead you to change your mind even on major issues.

The most important question is clearly where the relevant conversations are happening and, relatedly, which of the journals concerned is most likely to welcome what you have to say. It follows that you will be citing works from the target journal or journals. It is frankly amazing how many researchers approach the subject of where to submit their work without having immersed themselves in reading the journal they are going to send their work to. All too often, researchers are led first of all by considerations such as journal ratings (discussed below) and ideas about whether the journal is 'easy to get into' according to their friends and immediate colleagues. My advice is to put ideas about 'easy to get into' aside and to focus on where your article is likely to appeal to readers, reviewers and editors because of a prior interest. Above all, study the journal very carefully, see what its concerns are, what its articles actually look like and take the trouble to read the notes for contributors. A very functional rule to apply is to think about who your article might be sent to for review because these people's work should be very carefully cited and you should think how they might react to your work.

You should also take into account the various sources that indicate a journal's quality. There is a whole industry purporting to categorise journal quality and I only offer the most basic of guides here since (a) it is such a massive field and (b) there is more to our subject than these metrics, as I argue below. Some famous journals need no introduction and this already tells us something. Celebrated journals such as *Academy of Management Journal*, *Modern Law Review*, *American Economic Review*, *Human Relations* and *Past and Present* make the point for me. Outside of this sort of world-famous journal, one useful indicator of status will be the journal's 'Impact Factor', an indicator of how often articles in a journal have been cited elsewhere. A rule of thumb I use is that an IF of 1.0 or above is broadly acceptable if you are aiming at a 'respectable' level. Journals publish their IF on their web sites because they have to pay to acquire one and are very unlikely to fail to publicise it when they have paid for it. However, not all journals have IFs; if they do not give one on their site it is almost certain they do not have one. It is important to see what Impact Factors do and do not guarantee: they do show a journal's resonance in the research community and, by extension, their reputation; what they do not guarantee is that any particular article will be widely cited. Widely-cited articles come from journals with very different quality ratings and many articles in journals with high Impact Factors have very little measurable resonance in citation terms. Therefore, you need to take measures to raise your citations quite independently of the journal and I deal with this at the end of the book.

There is also a wide range of journal quality guides issued by various bodies including that issued by the British Association of Business Schools, which is effectively the 'industry standard' for measuring journal quality both in Britain and increasingly more widely in Europe. There you will find a set of star ratings with top international journals rated 4, down to the lowest level of 1. Journals rated 4 can also be sub-divided: if the journal is considered to have a claim to be part of the 'World Elite' then the number of authorities with that view will also be given and anything at or above a rating of 1 is clearly good. Again, if the journal you are looking for is not in the list it is because it is rated 0. Some institutions also have their own ratings lists, which will count for something in the institutions that produce them. Outside of those institutions they do not count for very much however, simply because they generally reflect the journals edited or preferred by influential members of the institution's senior staff and are therefore not 'industry standard'. That is not to say they should be entirely ignored, but too much weight should not be given to their ratings. We should also note here that any journal which is actually asking for articles (such as most of the commercially-driven 'open access' publications) should be approached with a strong dose of scepticism. 'Open access' is a seductive term but many journals (like many conferences) have grown up as purely commercial operations to meet the demand for publication which have no standing in the academic community and here journal ratings lists are helpful as they show journals' real standing. The commercial 'open access' journals have been described by one authority as 'predatory' (Harzing, forthcoming). You should ask senior colleagues if in doubt.

Once you have determined the journal's broad quality, you will be asking questions about whether it is best to aim (very) high or to be more modest in your initial ambition. You should not be naive about this. It is unrealistic for the overwhelming majority of early career researchers to submit their work to any of the famous journals named above with any real hope of success. These journals all have rejection rates of at least 90% at any given point in time. Relatively inexperienced authors are only likely to stand a chance if they have top co-authors simply because writing this sort of article requires capacities that are generally only developed across many years. This 'rule' may also sometimes be broken by individuals writing on very 'hot' topics. Nevertheless, some submit to these journals without much real prospect of success simply because they are told by all around them 'that is the best' and understandably do not want second-best. The probable result of submitting to these journals and others of the very highly rated sort will be rejection, possibly if you are lucky with a line or two from the editor saying why s/he does not consider the article worthy of review. The problem is that in some cases this can lead to delays before an article is seriously considered. A second problem may be your own morale. We all have to pay attention to our own emotions and it is difficult to live on a diet of constant rejection. Success stimulates self-confidence and breeds further success; its absence diminishes them.

A much better result will be rejection after reviews as in this case you will receive valuable criticism. Top journals (typically those which at least someone considers part of the 'World Elite') often provide excellent feedback that can be used to help you revise your work and submit elsewhere. North American journals often provide very good and extensive reviews if you can get to this stage (i.e. get past the desk rejection stage, see below), partly because their doctoral students are trained to give this sort of criticism and partly because it is expected by editors. The strategy you adopt needs to be realistic and my working criterion would be the following: if an experienced researcher in your field reads your article and feels it has a good chance of a 'revise and re-submit' verdict from a journal then that journal is a worthwhile target. A realistic choice of target journal, together with a good piece of work, given sympathetic reviewing, should result in a 'revise and re-submit' decision. This is a great result; very few articles are simply accepted as they are. You will now be in a (hopefully constructive) dialogue with the journal and its reviewers/editors.

When you are deciding on a target journal, there are several factors worth taking into account which go beyond the journal's ratings and reputation. The first is the sort of approach it takes to different types of work and also to how they deal with authors. Journal web sites may be useful in respect of the types of research approach they prefer to read and accept, but they can also be misleading; although some say that they do not favour particular approaches, a brief look at the articles they publish often shows that this is either untrue or that they are simply not sent more than one or two particular types of work. The other central issue is how they deal with authors, or what I call their all-round 'offer' to those who submit to them. Journals' 'offers' to authors are not always entirely consistent (they may well vary between different editors and reviewers) but they often show a certain uniformity. Advice has to be taken from senior colleagues as to recent experience with the journal in question, but there are several key questions they should be asked: (1) Does the journal tend to 'desk-reject' a high proportion of articles? – desk rejection means the article is rejected by the editor soon after receipt. Desk rejections can often run at 50% of the articles submitted. (2) Is it normal for the editors to take a developmental approach with authors whereby they are prepared to work with them to improve an article, or is it one which tends to dispense summary justice? (3) How prompt is the journal in replying to initial and subsequent versions of the work (an area in which journal web sites can be poor guides)? One way of finding out how fast journals work to turn articles round is to study the details provided by some of them on recently published articles. These state the claimed dates of initial submission and final publication. Although these dates are in my experience not always accurate, there are limits to how far these dates can be manipulated by journals trying to look more attractive to authors.

Another significant consideration that goes beyond ratings and metrics is how well the journal is distributed; journals will tell you this on their websites and since they do not tend to understate, you can make comparisons. The top journals tend to be very well distributed and subscribed to by university libraries that can afford their normally high rates everywhere in the world, but some less highly-rated journals are also well diffused internationally. It bears repeating that insistent e-mails asking that you publish in a recently-founded 'open access' journal edited by a small group of scholars are probably best-ignored despite their 'open' claim. Another consideration is whether journals have a strong publisher behind them. A further one is the national scholarly traditions of the country in which the journal is published. The main choice here is between American and European-based journals. These have certain distinct characteristics which come from their respective scholarly traditions. First, American-based social science and business and management journals have a strong tendency to prefer quantitative work; qualitative work, when it appears in their pages, is generally of extremely high quality and has clearly imposed itself. This is much less true of European-based journals. Second, in all disciplines and fields of study covered by this book, American journals tend to dislike sharp criticism of established authorities. This is also much less true of European-based journals, some of which have traditions of robust debate. Third, previously well-established journals published in languages other than English—we think here of German and French language journals in particular such as *Geschichte und Gesellschaft*, *Emploi et Travail* and so on are increasingly finding life difficult. This has led them to allow authors to write or at least to provide English-language abstracts with their German or French texts. In some cases (such as the German-language journal *Arbeit*, for example) it simply allows authors to write in English. Increasingly, therefore, they provide an excellent way of reaching certain national audiences.

Submitting an article to a special edition of a journal is one of the ways that early career researchers often manage to place their work. This is because the competition is limited to those with an interest in and something to offer in a restricted subject area. Knowing about special editions, when they are going to make their call for articles and exactly how much latitude the special edition editors are going to allow authors is when the quality of your networking is likely to be relevant. Special edition editors want sufficient quality articles that make contributions across a particular set of sub-topics or geographic regions. Having proposed the special edition, they will want to avoid a situation where they have too few good quality articles or have a few that are bunched into just one of a number of sub-topics. They will therefore try to ensure sympathetic reviewing and to help authors when necessary rather than simply act as strict gatekeepers. Partly for this reason, it is often said that special editions tend to have less high quality articles than normal editions of any journal. On the other hand, if you produce a particularly attractive article that cannot be accommodated in the special edition, and the special edition editors pass it on to the general editors, it is far from unknown for these works to be published in one of the journal's normal editions. Another possibility is to submit your work to a recently-founded journal and to insert yourself before others have registered its existence. This may help you get your work published but you should be aware that experienced students of publication lists look out for this particular tactic, easily detectable from the journal edition number.

The choice of where to submit your work is in short a complex one, requiring great care and attention and guidance from senior colleagues, familiar not only with the journals but also with your work.

Drafting the article: the process

Writing articles may be understood as something other than simply a process of construction. It is also a learning process, whereby the author or authors explore and develop their analysis, ideas and interpretation with all of these different elements interacting, teaching themselves as they proceed. This has consequences in that it shows us the limits of planning. It may also help you to deal with the inevitable elements of frustration that occur when difficulties arise.

Before I launch into the specifics of drafting articles, I offer one general piece of advice on method that applies throughout: *write-talk-write-talk-write- talk-write*. As I suggested above, the writing process is one of self-education. It is also one that seeks to communicate ideas and analyses to others as clearly and unambiguously as possible. It is therefore best in my experience constantly to talk about the article at every stage, since talking will help you achieve both the learning and the clarity goals. The written can and should be furthered by the verbal. Writing and speaking are two very different forms of articulation that draw on different mental processes and result in different modes of expression. As you articulate verbally, so you will see flaws and problems with what you are saying and simultaneously, ideas for development will occur to you. You may object that you have no collaborator and that there is nobody else to discuss the article with, but normally there is some intelligent person available and willing to listen and to ask questions. They should be able to understand what you are arguing. If they do not, do not be tempted to hide behind statements like 'oh, they are not a specialist and would not understand'. Rather, ask yourself how the explanation could be clarified. Finally, the processes of verbal articulation are so important to good clear writing that you can read passages over to yourself if need be.

How might you go about drafting your article? There is no single right way but the way I work is to begin by mapping out ideas in a 'brainstorming' way on screen or on paper either alone or with others. Ideas are not ruled out at this initial stage but noted down so that they are captured before being dismissed as irrelevant to the way the planned article is developing. After that stage, I write an initial abstract as a working tool and guide to my work. The point of this abstract is to act as a statement of the article's central strengths and selling points, as a very basic map and an anchor for the article itself. This process forces you to think of what the selling points are, as without them your article is unlikely to find a home. The abstract should focus on contribution to the literature, not on the context, data, material, case or analytic method which is used within it. Although all of these other things might be included in the abstract's final version, at this early stage they can tend to divert you from the key task of identifying the contribution. It should also not go beyond 100-200 words as more will be too long for the sort of brief statement which is needed. Over-long initial 'abstracts' tend to provide authors with a lot of words which conceal the lack of serious selling points or theoretical contributions. Once this abstract has been created, it is probably wise to discuss it with your collaborators, a mentor or another colleague before going further. When you begin writing the article itself, the abstract and the article can develop in dialogue with each other. That is, when the initial abstract and the article start to look different in some major way, then one or the other needs to be changed. The point is that you do not lose sight of the overall plan or the article's main merit as you write.

Planning your article from beginning to end is clearly a sound idea. A simple bullet-point type of plan will be helpful after the initial abstract has been written. It bears repeating that the plan will have a lot of shortcomings and, like Napoleon's battle plans, will be promptly abandoned on contact with the enemy. At this stage, you need to pay serious attention to the keywords and title that you intend to use. These parts of the article will have a major role in attracting readers and therefore citers of your work. One way of initially identifying articles is of course the electronic word search; titles and keywords are of great importance here. You can get some indication of the keywords that most attract readers by entering them in Google Scholar. Titles should be brief, scholarly, faithful to the article's content and attractive, rather than over-long attempted summaries. One should probably try not to be too metaphorical in a title. If you use commonly-used phrases such as 'shifting sands' or 'see wood for the trees' in your title then you may attract readers with different concerns from those of your article who will soon realise their mistake and move on.

In establishing the finished article's appeal, the final abstract, introduction and conclusion are also crucial. Not only do they play a role in attracting and drawing readers in, they also provide brief guides to and summaries of the article, helping others to cite it. In many cases these parts can be problematic. This has consequences since they are the first things that the reader will encounter when they look at the article when they decide whether and if so how to read or skip-read it. They may, for example, decide that the article is only of marginal interest and read it quickly; in this case they will be less likely to cite it. The final abstract should state quite clearly what exactly the article is about rather than be-as some are-a sort of substitute for an introduction. It should not look like something done in a rush and without great care at the end of the writing process when the author is tired. It should present the central argument rather than the type of material or data the article uses (unless these are especially remarkable). It should try to link the article's subject to an important area of public and/or academic discussion or debate. The abstract needs to be closely linked to the introduction so that the reader moves from one to the other without encountering more than the necessary and worthwhile amount of repetition, and is drawn in. The introduction-like the conclusion-is an especially important part of your article. It is the last section that many authors write, because only when it is quite clear exactly what the article argues can it provide a good overview and the necessary context(s).

A good introduction should contain a clear statement of the article's subject area and follow that up by showing the subject's significance. In short, you should try to draw the reader into reading the article and seek to engage their serious attention so that they want to do more than skip-read it. The introduction should also-after doing the tasks suggested above-establish central definitions of the terms used and provide an overview of the article's overall structure. It may in some cases provide a rationale for the work. I now give an example of a very late draft of a title, abstract and introduction from an article I wrote together with my friend Didier Michel, which appeared in the *Journal of African Law*.

'Legal at the time'? The case of Mauritian slavery

Richard Croucher and Didier Michel

ABSTRACT

This paper critiques the 'legal at the time' argument used by states and companies which practised slavery, examining the Mauritian case. Most types of legal actions for restitution for slavery face formidable difficulties. Reparations may be a more viable route. Yet a central argument against reparations is that slavery was 'legal at the time'. We demonstrate that this argument is open to challenge. The years of historic rupture, 1794-1839, when the local élite defied first French and then English law, generated systemic unlawful activity. We also show that French constitutional law offers possibilities for legal actions in the form of rights that are not time-limited.

INTRODUCTION

We critique the 'legal at the time' argument used by states and companies involved in slavery and the slave trade, examining the case of Mauritius. We do so paying the necessary attention to historical context. Following Ariela

Gross, we seek to 'expose historical assumptions and narratives that oppose redress'[1]. As Gross herself demonstrates, legal judgements on slavery have frequently been informed by incorrect historical assumptions. This work therefore lies at the intersection of law and history.

We consider possible legal arguments available in French and English law, which if they concern those foreign states must be raised in France and Britain as Mauritian law requires[2]. Claims against companies may also be viable in Mauritius under these legal systems because of the continued application of both on the island. We envisage demands for reparation and specific legal actions without entering into much-debated definitional issues on reparations[3]. We simply conceptualise them as any form of material compensation from the descendants of those who benefitted from slavery to the descendants of those who suffered from it.

Demands for reparations and actions--for example for unlawful enrichment—cannot be clearly separated in terms of their legal foundations. We suggest that the broad political case for reparations may be supported by some of the legal bases referred to below. We conclude that since

---

[1] A Gross "When is the time of slavery? The history of slavery in contemporary legal and political argument" (2008) 96 *California Law Review* at 283-321.
[2] R Domingue "Legal method and the Mauritian Legal System" Réduit, University of Mauritius, 2003(25).
[3] For discussion of these complex issues, see T Craemer 2009; "Framing Reparations" (2009)37/2 *The Policy Studies Journal* at 275-298; S Kershnar "The inheritance-based claim to reparations" (2002)8 *Legal Theory* at 243-267.

actions have very limited possibilities of success, reparations claims may represent a more viable option.

The remainder of the article is structured as follows. First, we provide context on both the international and national debates before sketching essential detail on the history of slavery in Mauritius. Next, in the article's main body, we examine in turn possible legal bases for reparations claims against companies and ex-imperial states. Finally, we attempt to identify those grounds which appear most likely to succeed.

As suggested above, conclusions are also vital parts of an article and how they are written is therefore important. The conclusion deserves some substantial space since it is where the article's 'punch lines' are located, and is the culmination of your work. It should not be (as some are) too short or cryptic simply because the author has run out of space and energy. Above all, it needs to show the article's contribution to knowledge and to relate that to other work in the area. Many authors identify their contribution in weak ways. The most common misstep is to over-claim and say that the article achieves things that in fact it does not and/or are in fact established by other researchers. Another is for authors to call something a contribution when all they are doing is to re-state the research gap, along the lines of 'this article adds to the literature on xyz'. We should remember that simply adding to literature is not to make a constructive or progressive contribution to it.

Below, I reproduce the conclusion from the article whose abstract and introduction I gave above:

CONCLUSION

We have attempted to counter the important 'legal at the time' contention in the Mauritian case, an exercise that we suggest may also be conducted fruitfully for other countries. We put forward four key counter-arguments. First, the Dutch VOC executed alleged offenders without trial, which was unlawful at the time. Second, for some years after 1794, French law had abolished slavery but was rejected by the island's slave-owning élite despite their nominal adherence to French law. Third, and related to the previous proposition, at French law the right to liberty is inalienable, has been since the DDHC, and claims that it has been breached cannot be time limited. Fourth, false imprisonment was an offence at English law well before the 19th century and appears to have occurred during 'apprenticeship'. The arguments encompass both specific events and periods and the broader phenomenon of slavery and the slave trade, post- French Revolution. They may be strengthened by further documentation which may be provided by the TJC and through work in the Mauritian National Archives and elsewhere. Nevertheless, we contend that slavery was not always 'legal at the time'.

Our propositions counter the argument advanced by some anti-reparations scholars[4] that demands for reparations

*are automatically flawed because they necessarily involve
a counter-factual, i.e. comparison of a world without
slavery (which cannot be observed) with the actual
historical situation. They cumulatively also suggest that
ground should not be too readily conceded to the 'legal at
the time' argument in any national context.*

*Normally, laws were instituted that allowed profit-
maximisation by means acceptable to élites. Yet the law
and its formal terms must always--and here slavery is far
from an exception--be located firmly within the context of
wider social relations. Under slavery, power relations
were such that slave owners could act largely without fear
of consequences. In the Mauritian context, the slave
owners broke even the terms of the Code Noir which it
could be argued did little more than codify their interests
as property owners. They rejected the French Revolution's
legal challenge. Then, when the slave owning élite wished
to reject British 'amelioration' laws, they referred to the
unusual terms of the compromise negotiated when the
British took over. In short, they then referred to the status
of French law (which had crucially changed in content) on
the island. They confined ex- slaves to their estates under
the transitional 'apprenticeship' arrangements. Thus,
while Noël argues that slave abuse was not systematic
under French rule, this tends to obscure the fundamentally*

---

[4] See for example, S Kershnar "The inheritance-based claim to reparations"
(2002)24 *Legal Theory* at 243-267.

unlawful nature of the practice of slavery in the decade after 1794 and indeed beyond.

A case appears to exist against companies operating slavery and the slave trade unlawfully in the years immediately after 1794 on the ground of unlawful enrichment. A case against France for injuries arising from its failure to enforce the DDHC may also exist. A (probably smaller) possibility also exists of cases under the Loi Taubira since it remains unclear despite affirmations to the contrary whether such a law can deny individuals rights and therefore operate against slaves' descendants material interests. Whether its essentially declaratory nature will serve to raise the profile of slavery and the slave trade and thereby both raise incentives and provide grounds for descendants to make legally-based demands or, on the other hand, simply block them remains uncertain. Legal arguments based on unlawful-at-the-time false imprisonment may have some purchase in English law, but the French civil law tradition appears to offer better prospects since it is more rights-based, transparent and clearly codified.

If the defence that slavery was 'lawful at the time' is at least questionable, it may prove inadequate for states and companies alike seeking to defend themselves against demands for reparations. Redress may be made by companies anxious to avoid negative publicity in the era of 'Corporate Social Responsibility'. Companies and indeed others may ultimately be judged in the court of public opinion, where norms and politics play a larger role than in legal contexts. Nevertheless, historical-legal arguments such as those we advance may have purposes that transcend the boundaries of the legal system itself, by playing a part in mobilising opinion.

Beyond their introductions and conclusions, articles will have a range of formats and approaches depending on their subject matter, their strengths and the expectations of the disciplines or fields of study they contribute to. I nonetheless give some pointers which may be helpful in drafting articles of any type. The first is that their structures should have a logical progression and, importantly, a balance between the different sections that fits what you are trying to achieve. Occasionally, sections can run away and become too large for the article's purpose. A good example of this is often that section which presents analysis of data; a common statement from researchers working in social science or business with qualitative data is 'I had to get all my data in' when of course all that is needed is enough well-chosen data to establish your key points. It is not about 'getting all your data in' but the dilemma you face is that of writing in enough depth and detail to convince your reader of the points you are trying to make. This is a matter of good data handling.

There are also two key qualities that articles need irrespective of field: focus and clarity; I now deal with these related characteristics in turn. *Focus* refers to a relentless and exclusive attention to the problem under discussion. All too often, articles lack the sense of ruthless focus that pushes the writer to penetrate to the heart of issues; they digress constantly, obscuring the logic of the argument they are trying to develop and verbal 'clutter' is littered all over the article at every level: the sentence, the paragraph and the article levels. 'Clutter' or unnecessary words and phrases need to be relentlessly pruned, to expose the central discussion. The end result of poorly-written work littered with clutter is often an article that is over-long both in terms of the journal's word limits and also in terms of the value of what the article actually has to contribute. Focus is closely related to the second important characteristic: *clarity*. Clarity can be divided into two (again closely related) types: conceptual and textual/linguistic clarity. The first-conceptual clarity-refers to the ways that the key analytic concepts are defined and used in the article, while the second refers to the clarity of what is said at the sentence, paragraph and article levels. Too many researchers write in over-long, convoluted sentences that obscure rather than elucidate meaning. Sentences should be short and not have several sub-clauses. Paragraphs should follow the old advice: *one paragraph, one subject*. If it helps the author, it may be worthwhile assigning a title to each paragraph that can later be deleted until the 'one paragraph, one subject' rule becomes habit.

Focus and clarity are difficult to achieve and when they are, the result may appear deceptively simple to the reader because the logic is compelling. The only way I can achieve this is through constant drafting and re-drafting. At the end of a period of re-drafting, I then find it best to set an article aside for a period typically of at least a fortnight so that I can achieve 'distance' from the article. When I have done that, I can return to it and see it much more objectively than after a period of intensive writing at the end of which I have become too close to it. After a fortnight or better still a month I can edit the piece much more easily. In some cases, whole sentences or even passages containing detailed analysis or argument are abandoned. I put these in a separate file labelled 'scrapyard: name of article'. Before I finalise the article I look around the scrapyard to see if anything can be salvaged from it and used in the main text.

After a number of rounds of revision you should feel you have come to the end of what you can usefully do. A good sign of having reached this point is when you start to think that the revisions you are contemplating are not necessarily improvements on the previous text. At that point, it is time to seek out a few friendly reviews from your colleagues, mentor and other people who are prepared to help you in this way. The quality of the feedback you will get will of course partly depend on the amount of effort they put into it and the honesty they show. An easy way out taken by some senior people is to provide minimal feedback, saying 'that is excellent, I suggest you send it to (name of top journal in the field)'. Beware of that type of feedback. The quality of the feedback will also depend on how well you brief them; if there are specific aspects of the article that concern you or in which their opinion is especially valuable, then they should be asked specifically to comment on these. However, it is not a good idea to ask them *only* to comment on these rather than on the entire article because authors very often misdiagnose the real issues with their own work.

When you are close to being ready for submission, it will be important to find and work with a reputable academic editor. We all need our editor, i.e. someone to come at the work from another angle, to ask us why we say things in particular ways and to point out alternative ways of expressing ourselves in order to improve focus and clarity. Many researchers make the mistake of thinking of this as simply 'proof-reading'. Proof-reading articles will improve the reader's overall impression of the care with which the whole work is being presented and editors do not want to do this themselves. *Editing* goes further than proof-reading to address more serious issues. Poorly-edited work undermines the authority of the text. It has unfortunately become increasingly the norm in some journals, and hardly improves the reputations of those journals, nor of the authors appearing in them. When I refer to academic editing, I am not referring simply to proof-reading, but to a much wider and vital academic role:

that of the academic editor, who will question structure and obscurity of expression wherever s/he encounters it. When I look at an article for the first time if I am editing a journal, an important question I ask is of course 'how much fiddly work will I have to do on it?' I am not very happy if the answer is 'quite a lot'. The author of the article has in that case created some prejudice against him or herself.

Articles obviously have their own fundamental contributions, strengths and weaknesses and these are ultimately what count. They also frequently have a combination of signifiers that provide clues about their quality. The analogy here is with a second-hand car; its fundamentals may be good or bad, but it will also have superficial things you would look out for as the potential purchaser such as how clean the windscreen is. The common objection is 'well these so-called signifiers are not what is important about the article' and that is true. But it also remains true that they are in practice strongly associated with the things that *are* important. I list the signifiers of strong and weak articles below.

Signifiers of a strong article

Written in good academic English

Well within the journal's word limit

Crisp, attractive, well-written abstract

Conceptual clarity, structural clarity and clarity of expression

Entirely consistent in its use of terms

Progresses logically

Focused discussion

Each section and paragraph is effectively linked

Derives, presents and answers a clear research question

Good mini-summaries at the end of each section

Tables and figures are appropriately labelled and linked to text

Makes only proportionate, measured and convincing claims for its contribution and significance

References and/or footnotes are in good order; both they and the text follow the journal's guidelines at submission stage

Signifiers of a weak article

Constantly repeats stock phrases such as 'this article contributes to the literature on x'

Weak identification of gaps in previous work

Levels of headings are unclear and inconsistent

Tables and figures poorly or even unlabelled

Constantly shifts between different terms and between different versions of what it describes as the article's main focus, contribution and so on

Vast tracts of non- or only semi-analysed material

Long lists of references to support very well-established and obvious statements where a reference to a review article or two central authorities would suffice

Abstract reads more like an introduction, is vacuous and omits contribution that matches article

Introduction is over-long and is little more than background information

Rambling and unfocused conclusion. An alternative in this kind of article is a very short conclusion where it appears the author has run out of interest or energy

Submitting the article

There is always a question about whether an article is ready to send off to the journal you have targeted. One way of having an idea about whether you have done the best you can with it is one I introduced above: the point at which changes you make to the text appear as questionable in the extent to which they are improving it. Another is probably better because it is less subjective: to ask the question of friendly reviewers, so that you have an external expert opinion. There are those who submit an article when they themselves do not feel it is finished (for example, with only semi-finished formulations and references), so that they receive feedback from that journal at a relatively early stage; journal editors are aware of this and as the pressure on journal editors' time increases, it does not predispose them to treating such authors sympathetically. Once you have decided to send it off, if it is collaborative work, all authors should be given a final chance (clearly flagged up as that) to look through it before submission. Everyone needs to agree the title and keywords that will be used to describe the article. On those unusual but not unknown occasions when the journal invites authors to name their reviewers to provide supplementary reviews to those which the editor will obtain, the authorial team will need to agree who to name and make sure they are contacted before submission so that the invitation to review does not come as a surprise to them. The same applies where the system invites authors to name reviewers that they would *not* like the article to go to. The electronic submission system may-depending on the journal-also give you the opportunity to write a covering letter to the editor and you need to think carefully together about whether this will be a good idea or not. Sometimes it can be a good idea to try to head off certain individuals from being invited to review where there are legitimate reasons (for example when that reviewer's work is directly criticised or when s/he has publicly announced that s/he is out of sympathy with the approach you are taking). You should think very carefully about anything the editor needs to know about the article but do not waste their time either. There are some things that early career researchers rather like saying in these letters that are almost certainly best avoided. The most common is 'this is the result of my doctoral work' because some regard that as meaning that the person concerned is inexperienced at this level.

When all of the authors are happy to see the article submitted, someone clearly has to submit it. Many authors dislike frustrating electronic submission processes and the tedious work involved and therefore ask someone more junior to do it. This is a separate job from naming the corresponding author and it is probably not a problem to have a junior corresponding author, it is probably best on the other hand if that person is a senior member of the authorial team in order to underline the team's weight. In most cases, when the submission has been made, all of the authors are informed by the journal's electronic system. Where this is not the case, the author handling the submission needs to inform everyone and to make sure that all authors have two copies of the article: one as submitted and the second in the version created by the electronic system (the page numbers and other details often vary due to re-formatting into a PDF by the system).

You are now awaiting feedback, but what do you do until that arrives? Most journals have article tracking systems, which are not usually very informative at all. Some simply say things such as 'received'; 'awaiting editorial consideration' or 'awaiting reviewers' feedback'. Some authors become quite agitated if the journal takes more than a few months to get back to them, especially if they are used to the fast feedback that is customary with British law journals (where weeks and even days rather than months are the norm). They may refer to the times published on the journal's website and then send off a mail to the editor protesting. It is probably not a good idea to do this unless the time taken from submission to feedback is more than four or five months as it is only likely to annoy the editor and/or to lead to summary justice being dispensed.

Receiving and responding to journal feedback

Introduction. Feedback from journals is likely to appear on the corresponding author's computer screen with a title such as 'Decision on MS reference number….' Reading and evaluating the feedback is now upon you. It is normal for the editor to use a standard format for his/her reply and to insert appropriate text into the format, to include the reviewer's comments and to invite you to submit a revised version by a certain date. The alternative will probably be wishing you all the best with your submission to another journal, hoping that the feedback will help you to develop the paper further and finally expressing the hope that you will consider the journal for your future submissions etc., etc.

Obviously, different types of feedback will be encountered over a career. One that poses no big problems is very positive feedback. Very few articles are simply accepted in the form they were submitted, but in that happy event, congratulations are indeed in order. In the event of this sort of reaction from a journal, it is probably best to simply be pleased rather than to ask yourself and any co-authors if you aimed too low in terms of journal (or even to ask 'is it really that bad a journal?')! Very good feedback does not always lead to publication and may even be designed to sugar a rejection pill. You can have a good article (especially for a special edition) but if the editor considers another one better, s/he may not have room for it and feels they have to reject it; it may for example be good, but not have good synergies with other articles in a special edition.

The alternative is much more common and it is as well to remember that most feedback is intended not to praise the work, but to improve it and therefore focuses on that aspect. Many researchers have a possibly sub-conscious mental model of feedback to undergraduates or at least students in their minds when they think of feedback, but this is inappropriate and even unfortunate when facing peer review, which is quite different. A sample quotation from one colleague faced by very critical comment on her paper serves as an example: 'surely there was something good about it?' This kind of comment has to some extent been taken heed of by some reviewers who claim to embrace the spirit of 'positive reviewing' but it also reveals the student marking model in operation.

The editors' commentary is the part of the decision letter which is of paramount importance. It is the editor who takes the real decisions, not the reviewers, who are there to advise. Sometimes editors do not balance their feedback very well, by which I mean they can do things such as deliver a broadly constructive message but in such a negative way that it can be hard to discern. I well remember sitting despondently with three co-authors as we contemplated some really rather negative commentary by an editor until one of our number pointed out that the editor nowhere said the article had been rejected. When the article was extensively re-drafted, it was pronounced fine and accepted without further amendment. On occasions, any amount of close reading of what the editor writes does not help. Editors may 'sit on the fence' and provide insufficient, unclear or inadequate guidance in relation to their reviewers' comments. Many early career researchers are often surprised to see that two reviewers often give very different or contradictory criticism. That is not surprising, but it *is* surprising when an editor simply tells them to meet the reviewers' comments. Wherever there is any doubt, authors should not hesitate to seek greater clarity from editors.

Rejection. Reading the feedback may be a difficult and painful experience if you have received a rejection especially if the feedback is particularly negative, hostile or even offensive. The latter is less uncommon than it should be. Some reviewers, behind the cloak of anonymity, may write things that could easily be re-phrased to be less likely to give offence (I have seen some quite bad examples of this sort of behaviour, which can only be described as nasty). We can only speculate as to their motives, or to the personality type that sees fit to behave in this way. It is unacceptable and I see no reason why you should not complain to the editor if you receive a bad case of it, because it is not increasing the likelihood of you submitting your work to that journal again. Rejection, especially when combined with this type of comment can be devastating at an early stage of a research career. This is an important turning point; some researchers find it very difficult to recover from a setback at the beginning of their careers; the same people find it much easier later in their careers when their rejection rate is not 100%. Strategies for managing your emotional as well as your intellectual response will therefore be relevant. First and foremost among these will be to realise that all researchers I know, including some eminent scholars, have been rejected. I have been rejected. You are not therefore alone. Second, you need to share your emotions with supportive people around you including of course any collaborators; this should not include any people who you are not entirely positive will demur from publicising your rejection among your scholarly peers in a bout of Schadenfreude. Third, it may be a good idea to print the feedback out and put it in a drawer until your negative emotions have subsided; there is a symbolic value in putting the document in its physical place and you will probably be in a better state to approach your response rationally after a week or so.

If your article was rejected, it is normally worth taking some time to revise it before sending it elsewhere if only because the same reviewers may see it again but also because feedback is valuable and should be used. Some articles suffer rejection time after time, being rejected by a range of journals in short order. This is as clear an indication as you can have that something is wrong and needs attention, even though there are those who constantly re-submit the same article despite this. The tactic might eventually succeed but the chances are low, and meanwhile you are burning up editorial goodwill quite fast.

Even when you have no need to overcome the worst emotional effects of rejection, you will need to set about revising your article before too long so that you do not eat too much into your revision time. In either case, how you approach the journal's feedback will be important. Many researchers' first reaction to criticism by journals is effectively to reject it often on the grounds that these people 'have no idea' and so on. It is also sometimes said that the rejection happened because the authors are not part of the reviewers/editor's network or clique. Understandable as it is, this sort of reaction is unfortunate and needs to be overcome. Ultimately, the editor(s) want to publish good research to raise the reputation of their journals and with it their own status in the research community.

Revise and re-submit. Our aim is to receive a 'revise and re-submit' and I now deal with this type of decision and how you can react to it. I obviously cannot simply reproduce feedback received from journals verbatim. I therefore reproduce below a pastiche made up from different editorial responses to several articles I have written in the business and management field. I take a worst case scenario from within the 'revise and re-submit' genre as this helps me to highlight some important subjects and also allows discussion of the maximum number of potential issues.

Dear Professor Croch

Many thanks to yourself and your co-authors for submitting your article to the Journal of Extremely Obscure Management Studies. I sent your work to two anonymous expert reviewers and attach their comments below, supplemented by my own. While they and I see some merit in your work, there are a number of serious issues to be addressed before I can consider your article again for publication in our journal. You will understand that the Journal of Extremely Obscure Management Studies has a very high quality threshold, a reputation acquired through the inputs of our authors, reviewers and editors over several decades.

Reviewer 1 felt that while your article may eventually have some interest for practitioners, it currently lacks a solid theoretical foundation and in particular that the derivation of the hypotheses needed further justification and indeed to take account of certain works which you have overlooked. R1 feels that this has impacted the hypothesis formulation and therefore had a potentially distorting effect on your results.

Reviewer 2 raised the issue of the data that you used. The data were drawn from single respondents in each company, and this means that the data are not reliable. You will need to take account of this real issue in some way in any re-draft.

For my part, my role has been to read your article not with a view to reviewing it in the same way as the two expert reviewers, but mainly to ensure the quality of what is published in our journal. I concur with the expert reviewers and have decided to give you the opportunity to revise your article. I invite you to submit a revised version addressing their comments while keeping within the journal word limit, but must warn you that this is a high-risk revision in view of the substantial nature of the reviewers' comments. If you are willing to revise your article by three months from the date of this communication I shall consider it again and re-send it to the reviewers. Please show clearly in your re-submission how you have addressed their concerns, by using track changes and by appending a letter in which you detail exactly how you have responded and at precisely what point in the manuscript you have done so. Perhaps you would be so kind as to let me know if you intend to re-submit.

With many thanks for submitting your work to the Journal of Extremely Obscure Management Studies. The letter above indicates the parts of the extensive feedback from reviewers that the editor chose to highlight. The authorial group naturally took it seriously and acknowledged the force of the points: the derivation of the hypotheses was seen as being rather weak and the single-respondent criticism was one we had all encountered (and dealt with successfully) before. Systematic feedback from experts is a valuable commodity and we needed, as you will, to interrogate and embrace it. Reviewers and editors may not always express themselves as well as they might. You will need to look closely at what they are saying and to try to penetrate beneath the surface of their comments to get not only at their essence but to try to see if you can even get beyond that to the unwritten. Sometimes, this kind of approach can lead one to suspect that there is more to the reviewers' criticisms than is explicitly stated. This might lead you to make changes that were not immediately obvious from the comments made by the rejecting journal's editor or reviewers. For example, in the case I use above, it was not simply a matter of deriving the hypotheses more thoroughly; reviewer 1 appeared not fully satisfied with the literature we were using and further searching brought us to other literature that allowed us to strengthen several significant arguments. We should have searched beyond the more obvious literature in the first place (a common fault, incidentally). In general, how well you react to criticism will be important to your chances of success. Although the peer review process can be painful, it generally improves the quality of outputs and contributes to our development. It is true that there may be some specific instances in articles when you look back years later and recall that you made a change you did not believe appropriate, but these will be the exception rather than the rule.

The communication from the editor reproduced above was received without great surprise. Exceptionally, it may be that you see feedback from journals as in some sense quite perverse or incorrect in important areas. This is rare, but it is also not entirely outside my experience. I have seen very detailed and convincing rebuttals of reviewer feedback where authors have taken a lot of time to refute many of the points and arguments made by reviewers. Many researchers do this in smaller ways with particular points they disagree with, but it can also be done on a bigger scale in relation to the entire article. You need to be very sure of your own ground to contemplate going into battle in this way, but it can be done in some cases by some people. In two cases I know, such replies have even led to an invitation to revise and re-submit. It is though a high-risk strategy because you may seriously upset the editor and it should probably only be done in extreme situations. Editors are powerful individuals in the research world, especially when they are sole editors; the constraints on them are normally few. Few editorial committees, scholarly societies or publishers exercise more than minimal elements of oversight over them.

When deciding how to deal with the feedback you will be faced with the question of how far down the path of accepting all their comments and suggestions you want to go. You will know the article and its logic better than reviewers and editors, and you may feel that some of their suggestions are not appropriate. Provided that you do something towards making most of the changes they request, there will not in most cases be an issue as long as you give a convincing argument about why you did what you did. There is a certain paradox involved here: although editors want you to improve your article, in general they do not require or in fact want your total obeisance. The article is yours and not theirs; it will have an underlying authorial voice and logic that you will probably understand better than they, which needs retaining. Most editors recognise this. I well remember reading feedback from an editor to a researcher after a first revision which summarises many editors' sentiments rather well (I paraphrase):

'You have dealt with the reviewers' requests in full. But please be aware that I do not see this as merely an exercise in compliance. It is your article. You still need to ensure the overall coherence of your article, and there is further work to be done in reinforcing that coherence in the light of the changes you have made.'

The point may become especially relevant as your article develops across a number of revisions and therefore changes quite a lot. Although some journals themselves limit the number of rounds of revision they are prepared to entertain (two or three is usual), some top journals will carry on more or less endlessly all the time they feel real progress is being made. This sometimes means that you can be rejected by top journals even after several rounds of revision if they feel that insufficient progress is being achieved. Though disappointing, this still leaves you with an article that has had a lot of external expert feedback, which may well be accepted by a less well-rated journal.

When re-submitting an article after revision, you should take every opportunity to communicate to the editor what you have done and why you feel it both meets the issues raised in feedback and how your revisions have maintained and built on the article's previous virtues. In addition, it is now common practice for people to use a grid like the one I show below to summarise your responses to feedback (remember that, as we suggested above there is more to revision than simple point-by-point response to feedback, useful though that is):

Comments by editor and reviewers (quotations)	What we have done and where including page and line number	Author's comments

The editor and reviewers should be thanked for their efforts. Many academics do not wish to review papers because they feel it brings them too little and they want to get on with their own research (which they then of course expect to be reviewed in timely fashion). Editors do derive some prestige from their position, but also attract opprobrium from some who have their papers rejected; conferences can be uncomfortable experiences for some of them). In any event, they are making efforts to improve your work and even if it only amounts to a few lines modifying a standard letter, they are doing something that few others do in our professional lives and deserve our thanks. A good guide to strategies for re-submission of articles to refereed journals is given by Yochanan Altman and Yehuda Baruch (2008).

Eventually, we hope that happy day will arrive when the article is finally accepted. The editor's letter will be quite explicit about this (the implication is that if you have not been told quite clearly, then the article is not in fact finally accepted). The editor may tell you then which edition it will be published in or at least give you a general idea of when the article will be put in the public domain, probably via the journal's 'on-line first' site. You may also be told when you and your co-authors will receive proofs for checking before publication. The proofs often come with a set of questions to the author from the journal's proof reader or copy editor and these may take some time to answer properly. These queries are quite often delivered with demands for an almost immediate turn-round in just a few days, which of course is not the best way to ensure that the proofs are in fact glitch-free. I have found that requests for a few days extra time are often granted and after all the effort that has gone in to the article it is a pity when authors do not have several sets of eyes going through the article looking to root out small issues. Surprisingly, it can often be the case that incorrect digits, symbols and vital words like 'not' appear (or not) in the wrong places even at this stage and this can be disastrous. You will probably soon be asked to sign a copyright assignment form assigning copyright to the publishers. After all the work that you have put in, you are asked to give up your copyright to a commercial publisher. I am aware of cases where authors have refused to sign this document and yet have still had their work published.

Publicising the article

First, I advise all authors to join the Authors' Licensing and Collecting Society, partly because it offers some possibilities for publicity but mainly because it collects copying fees for your work from around the world and sends you the proceeds once a year. It is worth it.

Once your article has been accepted, the process of publicising it and its findings begins. Do not assume that publication in a journal will mean that many people will read and cite your article. As I mentioned above, you cannot assume that publishing in a high-impact journal will mean that your article will be cited. Some people are very good at publicising their work. Others are less so, and rather tend to leave the article to publicise itself which is unlikely to happen. There are myriad ways of publicising your article and diffusing its findings and arguments. I do not attempt to deal with all of them here since it is a subject in itself, but simply draw your attention to the channels I regard as essential. It seems clear that a multi-channel approach is most effective. For further extensive treatment of these subjects, see Anne-Wil Harzing's various publications. The best guide I have found is the free online edition of her very useful book *Publish or Perish*, available at http://www.harzing.com/popbook/index.htm.

At around the time when your article was accepted, you should receive an offer to pay to have your article available to anyone who wishes to download the entire text free of charge. This is what is known in the UK as 'Gold

Open Access' (Gold OA). In other words, it means that readers and their institutions have immediate access to the publication without any further delay. Delays can be considerable if a library does not have the most expensive form of subscription to top journals, which typically stop researchers reading the most recent copies for (in some case) up to two years. This embargo system means that some researchers will not be able to use your work, or better put, will not be able to access it easily, for quite a long time. Typically, dealing with this problem through Gold OA costs anything between $1,000 and $6,000 per article depending on the publisher and publication. You need to read the precise forms of Gold OA that are being made available to you very carefully, to come to a decision about which, if any, you wish to choose. Some forms of Gold OA allow readers to make use of the text in more or less any way they like, which may not appeal to you. Some British universities pay this fee for you and it is a considerable benefit to the researcher or researchers involved. It is too early to state with certainty the extent to which this sort of access boosts citations as it has not existed for long enough. Nevertheless, I did a quick estimate of how it boosted full-text downloads of my own work by comparing a number of articles published in the same journal on broadly similar topics, some with and some without Gold OA. I found that it increased the monthly rate of full-text downloads by anything between 200 and 500%. These are downloads, not citations and the estimate is clearly very rough but the indications are positive.

'Green' Open Access (Green OA) is another form of Open Access that is more than helpful to have as a means of publicising your work. In the UK, it will be a condition of entry to the Research Excellence Framework 2020 that your publications have been available on Green OA since shortly after acceptance by the journal. Essentially, it means that the final version that you sent to the journal prior to proof-reading (i.e. not the entirely definitive version) is placed on a University's electronic research repository. Most British and many other universities have developed 'e-repositories' in recent years. These allow researchers to provide references to their published work and let readers download the version sent to the journal very soon after acceptance where this has been done by the author. The version published by the journal itself may also be placed on repositories after a period specified by the publishers. They are gradually becoming established as a very helpful way for researchers to keep up with the work of others. Therefore, the main difference between this and Gold OA is (a) the status of the version which readers may download and (b) the location and relatedly the visibility of the publication since with Gold OA readers scanning the journal itself will come across it through that channel.

Beyond these two key ways of making your work available, there are many other repositories/networks that publicise research publications such as ResearchGate, Academia.edu and Google Scholar that you can join and use. ResearchGate is a researchers' network as well as a repository of publications. Google Scholar is particularly easy and effective because you can join it easily and quickly and the Google Scholar system then searches for your publications and populates your entry with what it finds. You should consider joining research networks which also function as a publication exchange since they allow you to make your work available to the researchers in your tribe and beyond, to receive notification when their work becomes available, to publicise your profile and so on. These are considerable benefits. Some researchers also have other very effective personal methods of publicising their work. Probably the best of these is to keep a personal mailing list of key research contacts who you mail personally with a copy of your latest work, asking for any views they might like to share, a very direct means of keeping researchers around you aware of your outputs. You can also provide links to your recent articles as a footer to all your sent e-mails. Some researchers also maintain personal web sites.

Not the least benefit that many of these publicity methods provide is to give you ways of measuring and monitoring your own progress. One common way of measuring a scholar's academic impact is their 'H-Index'. This measures the number of articles produced, multiplied by the number of citations each has; you can calculate your own or simply refer to the figure for yourself published in Google Scholar. There are also other ways which you can use to monitor the progress made by your publications, by consulting Web of Science, ISI (much stronger in measuring relationships between articles in US-based journals) and Scopus (stronger than ISI on articles published in European-based journals). All of these invite you to register to be alerted when your work is cited and to see in this way who is working in a similar area to you. In some institutions, citations metrics must be provided in applications for promotion and even when not required, you can make use of it in that way. It may surprise you which of your works are most downloaded and, in due course, cited and by whom. This sort of information is not only helpful when applying for jobs or promotion but also help inform you as to which of your works are attracting most interest from certain audiences. This in turn may influence your publication strategy. Overall, the academic reach of your work may be measured by tools such as your rating on ResearchGate or by your H-index.

In short, many methods of measuring the influence of academic researchers' work on other academics that would have been justifiably been regarded as bizarre and even farcical by previous generations of researchers have been devised in recent years. They have been driven by states, managers and researchers. More will probably be devised. Ultimately, however, they are nothing more than simple indicators that cannot capture the intellectual merit of any work and it probably as well to remember that.

References

Jochanan Altman and Yehuda Barrach (2008) 'Strategies for Revising and Re-Submitting Articles to Refereed Journals.' *British Journal of Management*, 19(1), 89-101.

Richard Croucher and Didier Michel (2014) 'Legal at the Time? The Case of Mauritian Slavery.' *Journal of African Law,* 58(1): 89-108.
Sarah Delamont, 'Neopagan Narratives: Knowledge Claims and Other World 'Realities.' *Sociological Research Online*, 14(5). Accessed 23rd April 2014. <http://www.socresonline.org.uk/14/5/18.html>

Anne Harzing (2013) *The Publish or Perish Book: Your Guide to Effective and Responsible Citation Analysis.* Accessed 23rd April 2014. http://www.harzing.com/popbook/index.htm.

Anne Harzing, and Nancy Adler (Forthcoming in 2015) 'Disseminating Knowledge: From Potential to Reality – New Open-Access Journals Collide with Convention.' *Academy of Management Learning & Education.*

David Scott (2012) 'Research Designs: Frameworks, Strategies, Methods and Technologies,' in *Research Methods in Educational Leadership and Management*, Ann RJ Briggs, Marianne Coleman and Marlene Morrison (eds), London: SAGE. .

Streiner D and Sidani S (2010) *When Research Goes Off the Rails: Why it Happens and What You Can Do About It.* New York: Guilford Press.

Gary Thomas and David James (2006) 'Reinventing grounded theory: Some questions about theory, ground and discovery.' *British Educational Research Journal*, 32(6), 767-795.

David Tranfield, David Denyer, Palminder Smart (2003) Towards a methodology for developing evidence-informed management knowledge by means of systematic review *British Journal of Management* 14(3), 207-222.

David A. Whetten (1989) What constitutes a theoretical contribution? *Academy of Management Review* 14 (4), 490-495.

Printed in Great Britain
by Amazon.co.uk, Ltd.,
Marston Gate.

13400941R00058